Brett Favre

by Sharlene and Ted Nelson

Reading Consultant:
Dr. Robert Miller
Professor of Special Education
Minnesota State University

CAPSTONE
HIGH-INTEREST
BOOKS

an imprint of Capstone Press
Mankato, Minnesota

Capstone High-Interest Books are published by Capstone Press
151 Good Counsel Drive, P.O. Box 669, Mankato, Minnesota 56002
http://www.capstone-press.com

Library of Congress Cataloging-in-Publication Data
Nelson, Sharlene P.
    Brett Favre/by Sharlene and Ted Nelson.
    p. cm.—(Sports heroes)
    Includes bibliographical references (p. 45) and index.
    Summary: Traces the personal life and football career of the quarterback for the
Green Bay Packers.
    ISBN 0-7368-0576-1
    1. Favre, Brett—Juvenile literature. 2. Football players—United States—
Biography—Juvenile literature. [1. Favre, Brett. 2. Football players.] I. Nelson, Ted W.
II. Title. III. Sports heroes (Mankato, Minn.)

GV939.F29 N44 2001
796.332'092—dc21
[B]   00-027233

Editorial Credits
Matt Doeden, editor; Timothy Halldin, cover designer and illustrator; Heidi Schoof and
    Kimberly Danger, photo researchers

Photo Credits
Active Images, Inc./Rich Cane, 6; Mitchell B. Reibel, 10; Hector Sierra, 27;
    David Graham, 38
Allsport USA, 20; George Gojkovich, 14; Allen Dean Steele, 18, 25; Jim Gund, 28;
    Jonathan Daniel, 31, 33; Tom Hauck, 34
AP World Wide Photos/David Rae Morris, 13; Charles Kelly, 23
SportsChrome-USA/Vincent Manniello, cover, 16; Rob Tringali Jr., 4, 9, 36, 41, 42

2 3 4 5 6 06 05 04 03 02 01

Table of Contents

CHAPTER 1

A Championship Game

It was January 26, 1997. Brett Favre walked onto the Superdome field in New Orleans, Louisiana. More than 70,000 fans filled the stadium. They had come to see the Green Bay Packers and the New England Patriots in Super Bowl XXXI (31).

Brett led the Packer offense onto the field for the Packers' first offensive drive. Head coach Mike Holmgren wanted Brett to throw a short, safe pass for the first play. Brett lined up behind his center. He looked across the field at the Patriots' defense. He saw that the

Brett Favre led the Green Bay Packers to Super Bowl XXXI in New Orleans, Louisiana.

defensive players had not lined up as he thought they would. A short passing play would not work against the defense.

Brett decided to call an audible. He changed the play and shouted "74 Razor" to his teammates. This code was for a long pass to wide receiver Andre Rison.

Rison ran down the field when Brett took the snap. Brett waited and then threw the ball downfield. Rison caught the pass and scored a touchdown. The Packers took a 7-0 lead.

In the second quarter, the Patriots held a 14-10 lead. Brett and the offense took the field at their own 19-yard line. As he lined up, Brett saw another chance for a long pass. This time, Antonio Freeman would be the receiver.

Again, Brett shouted the play to his teammates. He took the snap and threw a perfect pass to Freeman. Freeman ran 81 yards to the end zone. It was the longest passing play in Super Bowl history. It also gave the Packers a 17-14 lead.

Brett threw for two touchdowns and ran for one in Super Bowl XXXI.

Brett and the Packers held their lead over the Patriots. Brett ran for another touchdown and helped his team to a 35-21 victory. After the game, Brett leaped into the air. He hugged Holmgren. It was the moment Brett had dreamed of all his life.

About Brett Favre

Brett Favre is the quarterback for the Green Bay Packers. He wears uniform number 4. Brett began playing in the National Football League in 1991. He joined the Packers in 1992. Most football experts consider Brett to be one of the best quarterbacks in the NFL. He won the league's Most Valuable Player (MVP) award three seasons in a row (1995–1997). No other NFL player has won this award three times in a row. Brett also is the only NFL quarterback to pass for 30 or more touchdown passes five seasons in a row.

Brett also is successful off the field. He spends a great deal of his free time helping charities. Brett owns a restaurant called the Brett Favre Steakhouse in Milwaukee, Wisconsin. He even has a candy bar named after him. It is called the Brett Favre MVP Bar.

CAREER STATISTICS

Brett Favre

NFL Passing Statistics

Year	Team	Games	Comp%	Yds	TDs	Int	Rating
1991	ATL	2	0.0	0	0	2	0.0
1992	GB	15	64.1	3,227	18	13	85.3
1993	GB	16	60.9	3,303	19	24	72.2
1994	GB	16	62.4	3,882	33	14	90.7
1995	GB	16	63.0	4,413	38	13	99.5
1996	GB	16	59.9	3,899	39	13	95.8
1997	GB	16	59.3	3,867	35	16	92.6
1998	GB	16	63.0	4,212	31	23	87.8
1999	GB	16	57.3	4,091	22	23	74.7
2000	GB	16	58.3	3,812	20	16	78.0
Totals		145	60.8	34,706	255	157	86.0

CHAPTER 2

The Early Years

Brett was born October 10, 1969, in Gulfport, Mississippi. He is the second of Irvin and Bonita Favre's four children. Brett has an older brother named Scott and a younger brother named Jeff. Brett also has a sister named Brandy. She is the youngest of the Favre children.

Brett lived in Kiln, Mississippi, with his family. This small town is in southern Mississippi near the Gulf of Mexico. Bonita and Irvin both worked at nearby Hancock North Central High School. Bonita taught special education classes. Irvin coached the school's baseball and football teams.

Brett knew when he was young that he wanted to be an NFL player.

The Favre house was at the end of a dirt road. Brett's grandmother lived nearby in a mobile home. Both houses were near the edge of a bayou. Many wild animals such as alligators lived in this swampy area. Brett and Scott once threw cookies to three alligators near their house. A few days later, the alligators climbed out of the bayou. They crawled toward the Favres' house. Irvin thought they were looking for more cookies. He did not want alligators so close to his home. He chased them back into the bayou.

Grade School

Brett began playing sports in the first grade. He was 6 years old. He was tall and strong for his age. He played on a baseball team for 8-year-olds.

While in grade school, Brett helped his father during high school football practice. He pumped air into the footballs and carried water to the players. Brett liked to watch the high school quarterbacks throw the football.

Brett's parents are Irvin and Bonita Favre.

Brett played on his first football team in the fifth grade. He started as a receiver. In his first game, he caught a pass and fell on the ball. He could not breathe for several moments. Brett began to cry as soon as he could breathe again. He told the coach he wanted to play quarterback instead of receiver.

The coach let Brett change positions. Brett ran for two touchdowns and passed for another

A HERO'S HERO

NFL quarterback
Roger Staubach was
one of Brett's heroes
when he was young.
Staubach played
college football
for the U.S. Naval
Academy. He also
played quarterback
for the Dallas Cowboys. He led the Cowboys
to four Super Bowls.

Brett wanted to be an NFL quarterback
like Staubach. Brett liked to watch Staubach
play football on TV. Brett and his brothers
often played football in their backyard. Brett
sometimes pretended that he was his hero.

in his first game at quarterback. The people on the sidelines cheered. Brett knew then that he wanted to be an NFL quarterback.

High School

Brett was a star baseball player throughout junior high and high school. His high school team was called the Hawks. He pitched and played shortstop. He led the team in hitting all five years that he played.

Brett had mononucleosis when he was in the 10th grade. This disease made him weak. He also lost weight. He could not play football that year. Brett began to work out once he was well. He did push-ups and sit-ups. He also ate a healthy diet. He gained 25 pounds (11 kilograms). By spring, he was well enough to play baseball.

Brett was ready to be the Hawks' starting quarterback when he was in the 11th grade. Irvin was Brett's coach. Irvin preferred to have the team run the ball. Brett did not get to throw many passes. When he did pass, he

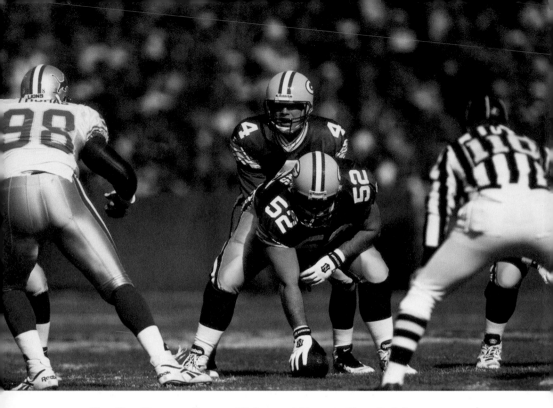

Brett often calls audibles while on the field.

threw the ball so hard that his receivers had trouble catching it.

In high school, Brett liked to do things his way on the football field. In one game, the score was tied with only seconds to play. The Hawks were on their opponent's 1-yard line. Irvin called a play. But Brett called an audible when he saw how the other team's defense was set. Brett kept the ball and dived across the goal line for the winning touchdown.

Brett did not only play quarterback for the Hawks. He also was the team's punter and place-kicker. He even played safety for the defense.

A Last Chance

Brett wanted to play college football. But few people outside Kiln knew how good a player Brett was. Newspaper reporters had not written about him. Coaches from large colleges had not seen him play.

One day, Mark McHale came to watch Brett throw. McHale was a friend of Irvin's. He also was an assistant coach at the University of Southern Mississippi (Southern Miss) in Hattiesburg, Mississippi. McHale watched Brett throw a few short passes. Then Brett threw a 65-yard pass. The pass proved to McHale that Brett could be a college quarterback. McHale helped Brett receive a football scholarship to Southern Miss. It was the university's last football scholarship for the 1987 season. Southern Miss had offered the scholarship to a different player first. But the other player decided not to attend Southern Miss.

CHAPTER 3

A College Quarterback

In late summer 1987, Brett left home to attend Southern Miss. The university's teams are called the Golden Eagles. People sometimes call them the Eagles for short.

The Seventh Quarterback

Brett's college coaches wanted him to play defense. They believed that he would make a good defensive back. Brett told his coaches that he wanted to play quarterback. But the team already had six quarterbacks. Brett would be the seventh-string quarterback.

Brett played college football at the University of Southern Mississippi.

Before the season started, Brett and the other first-year players practiced against the older players. He passed for two touchdowns in one of these practices. Brett's coaches liked what they saw. They moved him up to fifth string.

Brett continued to impress his coaches in practices. By the first game, he was the team's third-string quarterback. He traveled to Birmingham for a game against the University of Alabama. But Brett did not play. The Eagles lost the game.

A Great Start

The Eagles' next game was against Tulane University. The Eagles' top two quarterbacks played poorly in the first half. The team trailed 16-10 at halftime. The coaches decided to let Brett play. He was so excited that he almost threw up on the field.

Brett's first play did not gain any yards. But he then started to move the team's offense. He threw two touchdown passes. The Eagles won

---

Brett quickly became the starting quarterback for the Eagles.

34-21. After that game, Brett became the Eagles' starting quarterback. He was only 17 years old.

On Brett's 18th birthday, the Eagles played the Florida State University Seminoles in Tallahassee, Florida. The Seminoles were the highest ranked team in college football. The Seminoles beat the Eagles 61-10. The Seminole fans made fun of Brett by singing "Happy Birthday" to him. It was one of the worst losses of Brett's career.

Brett helped the team make up for the loss in the following weeks. He threw three touchdowns in each of the next two games. He finished the season with 14 touchdown passes. No Eagles quarterback had ever thrown that many touchdown passes in one season.

Continued Success

In his second season, Brett showed why he would someday be a great quarterback. In one game, the Eagles played the University of Eastern Carolina. Brett suffered from painful

Brett showed in college that he had the strength and speed to escape tackles.

leg cramps throughout the game. He could not run well. But Brett helped the Eagles keep the score close.

The Eagles trailed by four points in the game's final minutes. Brett knew his team needed a touchdown to win. He threw a 42-yard pass to bring the team to Eastern Carolina's 5-yard line. But he could not continue. His legs hurt too much to run down the field. He had to leave the game. Brett's backup came into the game and threw a short touchdown pass. The Eagles won 45-42.

The Eagles played Florida State again in Brett's third season. The Seminoles were again the highest ranked team in college football. Brett and his teammates remembered their loss to the Seminoles two years before. The Seminoles were favored to win the game easily. But Brett led his team to a surprising victory. He threw two touchdown passes during the game. His second touchdown pass came with only 23 seconds on the clock. It gave the Eagles a 30-26 victory.

The Accident

Brett looked forward to his last year in college. But he had an automobile accident in the summer of 1990. His car slid off the road and hit a tree. Brett was badly hurt. The accident had smashed the lower part of his stomach. In an operation, doctors removed 30 inches (76 centimeters) of his intestine. Football

Brett led the Eagles to a win over Florida State in 1989.

season was only a few weeks away. Brett's doctor thought Brett might not play football that season.

Brett missed the first game of the season. He had lost 34 pounds (15 kilograms). He was too weak to play. The next game was against Alabama. Brett told his coaches he was ready to play. Brett was still underweight. His uniform was baggy. But his return gave his teammates confidence. The Eagles beat Alabama 27-24.

Brett broke many Eagle records during his college career. These included the records for most passing yards and touchdowns in a career. Brett threw for a total of 8,193 yards at Southern Miss. He threw 55 touchdown passes. After his senior season, Brett played in the East-West Shrine Game. Many of the best college players in the United States take part in this game. Brett's team won. He was named the game's MVP.

Brett's experience in college prepared him for a career as an NFL quarterback.

CHAPTER 4

The NFL

After college, Brett knew he would be drafted by an NFL team. But he did not know which team. Three teams showed serious interest in Brett before the draft. These teams were the New York Jets, the San Francisco 49ers, and the Atlanta Falcons. The Falcons drafted him in the draft's second round.

Brett had a difficult rookie season with the Falcons. He was the team's third-string quarterback. He played in two games and threw only five passes.

Brett played his first professional season with the Atlanta Falcons.

To Green Bay

The Falcons traded Brett to the Green Bay Packers before the 1992 season. Ron Wolf had taken a management job with the Packers that season. Wolf had previously worked with the Jets. The Packers also had a new head coach. His name was Mike Holmgren. Holmgren had been an assistant coach with the 49ers. Wolf and Holmgren had both liked Brett before the 1991 draft. They agreed that Brett could be a great NFL quarterback.

Brett began the 1992 season as the Packers' second-string quarterback. Don Majkowski was the starter. But Majkowski hurt his leg in the third game of the season. This game was against the Cincinnati Bengals. Holmgren sent Brett into the game. Brett threw a touchdown pass with 13 seconds remaining. He led the Packers to a 24-23 victory. Brett became the Packers' new starting quarterback. He was only 22 years old.

Brett finished the season with 3,227 passing yards and 18 touchdowns. He was selected to play in the NFL Pro Bowl.

Brett proved his skills in a game against the Cincinnati Bengals in 1992.

Adapting to the NFL

Brett had a difficult season in 1993. He threw 19 touchdown passes. But he also was careless with the football. He threw 24 interceptions. Holmgren was unhappy with Brett's play. He thought Brett took too many chances. He told Brett to pass more carefully.

Brett continued to struggle in 1994. The seventh game of the season was against the

Minnesota Vikings. Early in the game, Brett threw an interception. He also hurt his hip and had to leave the field. Backup quarterback Mark Brunnel replaced Brett. Brunnel played well. After the Viking game, Holmgren thought about making Brunnel the starting quarterback. Some of the other coaches agreed. They believed that Brunnel could be more successful than Brett had been. But the Packers' quarterbacks coach Steve Mariucci convinced Holmgren to keep Brett as the starter.

Brett knew that he had almost lost his starting position. He began to play the way Holmgren wanted him to play. Brett took fewer chances. The team went on to win six of the next nine games of the regular season. Brett threw 24 touchdown passes. He threw only seven interceptions. He led the Packers into the playoffs. They beat the Detroit Lions in their first game. They then lost to the Dallas Cowboys. Brett was again named to the Pro Bowl.

Brett almost lost his starting position in 1994.

Brett had an even better season in 1995. He led the NFL with 4,413 passing yards and 38 touchdown passes. He also threw only 13 interceptions. He was named the NFL MVP. The Packers ended the season with an 11-5 record. They made the playoffs again. The team won its first two playoff games against Atlanta and San Francisco. But the Packers then lost again to the Cowboys.

Overcoming Addiction

Brett often was in pain during games. In a 1992 game, a tackler pulled on his left arm. Brett felt a pain in his shoulder. The team's doctor gave Brett a shot to ease the pain. Brett stayed in the game. The Packers won.

Brett also suffered bruises, sprains, and chipped bones during games. Brett began to take Vicodin pills. These pills lessened the pain. Brett soon began to use the pills even if he had no pain. Brett had become addicted to the drug. But Brett never took the pills on weekends when he had games.

Brett often must play with pain.

Brett won the NFL's MVP award for the 1996 season.

Brett was in a hospital after the 1995 season. Doctors removed bone chips from his ankle. Suddenly, he began to shake wildly. He then passed out. Later, the doctors told Brett that the Vicodin may have caused the problem. Brett was scared. He decided to stop using Vicodin. He went to a special clinic to overcome his addiction.

Super Bowls

Brett led the Packers to a 13-3 record in
1996. He threw 39 touchdown passes and 13
interceptions. Brett was again named the
NFL's MVP.

The Packers beat the 49ers in their first
playoff game. They then played the Carolina
Panthers in the National Football Conference
(NFC) Championship. The game was at
Lambeau Field in Green Bay. The temperature
was below freezing. Strong winds made the air
feel even colder. Brett never had lost a game in
that kind of weather. He threw two touchdown
passes in the first half. The Packers won
the game 30-13 and went on to win the
Super Bowl.

Brett wanted to repeat the team's success in
the 1997 season. He led the Packers to another
strong season. He again earned the NFL MVP
award. The Packers again made it to the Super
Bowl. But this time, they lost. The Denver
Broncos beat Green Bay 31-24.

CHAPTER 5

Brett Favre Today

Brett still is one of the best quarterbacks in the NFL today. But the Packers have struggled recently.

Disappointing Seasons

In 1998, Brett led the NFL in passing yards. The Packers reached the playoffs. But they lost to the 49ers in their first playoff game. The loss came on a last-second touchdown pass by 49er quarterback Steve Young.

In 1999, Holmgren left the Packers to coach the Seattle Seahawks. Ray Rhodes took his

---

Brett still is one of the best quarterbacks in the NFL.

place. The Packers finished the 1999 season 8-8. They did not make the playoffs. The Packers fired Rhodes after the season. They hired Mike Sherman to become the new coach.

Brett set an NFL record in 1999. On November 7, the Packers played the Chicago Bears. It was the 117th straight game Brett had started. No quarterback had ever started that many games in a row.

Brett's Family

Brett met Deanna Tynes when they were both in ninth grade at Hancock North Central High School. They began dating. The couple stayed together while they attended college at Southern Miss. Brett and Deanna married in July 1996.

Today, Brett and Deanna have two daughters. Brittany was born in 1989 while Brett and Deanna were in college. Breleigh was born in 1999. The family lives in Green Bay. They also spend time in Kiln.

Brett Favre Fourward Foundation

Brett is known for his love of children. He often visits children's hospitals in the Green Bay area.

Brett gives money to a variety of charities that help children.

He visits with sick children. He gives them shirts with his name and number.

Brett also helps run the Brett Favre Fourward Foundation. He gives money to Boys and Girls Clubs, the Special Olympics, and other charities through this organization. Golf is one of Brett's favorite hobbies. Every year, he hosts a golf match for celebrities. He uses the golf match to raise money for his foundation.

Career Highlights

1969—Brett is born in Gulfport, Mississippi.

1980—Brett plays quarterback on a grade-school football team.

1987—Brett graduates from high school and begins college at Southern Miss. He becomes the starting quarterback in the third game of the season.

1990—Brett ends his college career at Southern Miss; he holds the school records for passing (8,193 yards) and touchdown passes (55).

1991—The Atlanta Falcons select Brett in the second round of the NFL draft.

1992—Brett is traded to Green Bay. He becomes the Packers' starting quarterback in the fourth game of the season. He is named to the NFL Pro Bowl.

1994—Brett leads the Packers to the playoffs for the first time in 11 years.

1995—Brett leads the NFL with 38 touchdown passes and wins the NFL MVP award.

1996—Brett wins another MVP award. The Packers end the 1996 season by beating the New England Patriots in the Super Bowl.

1999—Brett sets an NFL record for quarterbacks by starting in his 117th straight game.

2001—Brett becomes the highest-paid NFL player when he signs a 10-year, $100 million contract with the Packers.

Words to Know

addiction (uh-DIK-shuhn)—a dependence on a drug or other substance

audible (AW-duh-buhl)—a play that a quarterback calls on the field; quarterbacks call audibles when they see that a coach's play will not work against a defense.

bayou (BYE-oo)—a stream that runs through a swamp and leads to or from a lake or river

intestine (in-TESS-tin)—a long tube below the stomach that digests foods and absorbs salts and liquids

mononucleosis (mon-oh-noo-klee-OH-siss)—an illness that causes a sore throat, swollen glands, and a high temperature; mononucleosis also is known as mono.

scholarship (SKOL-ur-ship)—a grant of money that helps a student pay for college

To Learn More

Dougherty, Terri. *Brett Favre.* Jam Session. Minneapolis: Abdo & Daughters, 1999.

Gutman, Bill. *Brett Favre: Leader of the Pack.* Millbrook Sports World. Brookfield, Conn.: Millbrook Press, 1998.

Mooney, Martin J. *Brett Favre.* Football Legends. Philadelphia: Chelsea House, 1997.

Savage, Jeff. *Sports Great Brett Favre.* Sports Great Books. Springfield, N.J.: Enslow Publishers, 1998.

Useful Addresses

Brett Favre
c/o Green Bay Packers
Public Relations Department
P.O. Box 10628
Green Bay, WI 54307-0628

Green Bay Packer Hall of Fame
855 Lombardi Avenue
P.O. Box 10567
Green Bay, WI 54307-0567

Pro Football Hall of Fame
2121 George Halas Drive NW
Canton, OH 44708

Internet Sites

CNN/SI—Brett Favre
http://sportsillustrated.cnn.com/football/nfl/
    players/1025

Green Bay Packers
http://www.packers.com

NFL.com
http://www.nfl.com

Web Celeb—Brett Favre
http://www.yahooligans.com/content/
    webceleb/favre

Index